Take~charge~of~ your~life Therapy

Take~charge~of~ your~life Therapy

adapted from
the bestseller *LIFE 101:*
Everything We Wish We Had Learned
About Life In School—But Didn't

edited by
Lisa O. Engelhardt

illustrated by
R.W. Alley

ONE
CARING
PLACE

Abbey Press

© 1995 St. Meinrad Archabbey
Published by One Caring Place
Abbey Press
St. Meinrad, Indiana 47577

Taken from the book
*LIFE 101: Everything We Wish We Had Learned
About Life In School—But Didn't,*
by John-Roger and Peter McWilliams,
© 1991 by Prelude Press, Inc.

Library of Congress Catalog Number
94-70290

ISBN 0-87029-271-4

Printed in the United States of America

Foreword

Do you sometimes feel that your life is careening out of control? Does it seem that other people or circumstances are running it for you? Do you wonder whether your life has any special purpose and how you are to discover it? Does your life seem flat, monotonous, *lifeless*?

If so, this small manual can help you get your life back on track.

The whimsical Abbey Press elves have joined forces with the wisdom of the bestselling book *LIFE 101: Everything We Wish We Had Learned About Life In School—But Didn't.* The result is a unique, delightful, and compelling guide to living and loving life that encourages you to take charge of your life by plunging in and experiencing it to the full.

If you want to learn to live, you must live to learn. So explore life around you and within you, the book advises. Don't be afraid to make mistakes; use them to enrich your life with self-knowledge and wisdom. You are the real teacher of the meaning of your life, as well as the student who must learn your life's lessons.

Take-charge-of-your-life Therapy points the way to a life that's full, fun, fulfilling, and fabulous. Live it up!

1.

Life is for doing, learning, and enjoying. The more you learn, the more you can do. The more you do, the more you can learn. Partake of your own life.

2.

Be an eager participator in life. Involve yourself; plunge in; embrace new experiences; experiment. Make your life an active science.

3.

Carry your riches within.
Wealth is being able to love
yourself fully. Wealth is
enjoying your own company.
Wealth is health, happiness,
loving, sharing, learning,
enjoying, and balance.

4.

Use everything for your enrichment, learning, and growth. No matter what happens to you, no matter how unfair or wrong, there's something you can take from the situation.

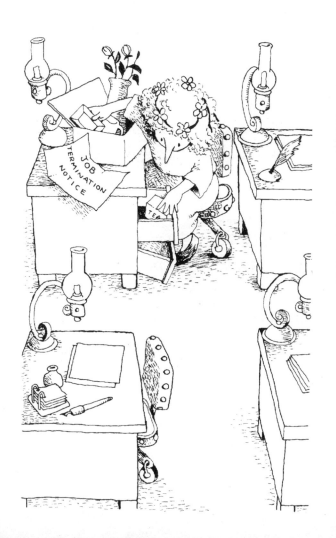

5.

Look within, be aware of your inner process, and stay open to the Spirit. If you listen carefully, you'll hear a voice inside yourself; it is the voice of your inner teacher. Its guidance is sure, clear, and direct. Pay attention.

6.

Life presents lessons to you.
You must decide, of all that
comes your way, what is true
and what is not, what applies
to you and what does not. You
are the real teacher, and the
learning is up to you.

7.

You have the power to take charge of the space within your own skin: your mind, your body, your emotions, your sense of y<u>ou</u>. Take charge of yourself.

8.

Take charge of your mind, being sure to keep it open. Your mind is an invaluable tool for sorting, organizing, conceptualizing, and replaying information.

9.

Strengthen your body. Get up, get moving, get going. Your body is your vehicle, like your car. Not giving your body direction is about as silly as letting your car choose its own course.

10.

Accept your emotions. If you're afraid of your strong feelings, like guilt, anger, disappointment, and fear itself, allow yourself to feel how afraid of those feelings you are. Then feel them anyway and, later, remind yourself that you survived.

11.

Build yourself a sanctuary—an inner retreat—in your imagination. It can contain anything or anyone you choose. You can change it or move it anytime. Here you can discover the truth about yourself.

12.

When you pray, imagine God's
love cascading over you like
pure, white light. It surrounds,
fills, protects, blesses, and heals
you—for your highest good and
the highest good of others.

13.

There is nothing you need to do
to become worthy; you already
are worthy. Worthiness has
nothing to do with action,
thoughts, feelings, mind, body,
emotions, or anything else. You
are worthy because you <u>are</u>.

14.

Your purpose in life has always been there. You've lived your life by it, perhaps without fully realizing it. It's your personal inner divining rod of truth. Discover your purpose.

15.

To find your purpose, make a list of all your positive qualities. Choose the two or three that suit you best and arrange them in sentences starting with "I" or "I am...." When you discover your purpose, it will "click."

16.

When you know your purpose, it's easier to choose and achieve goals. The litmus test of any action is simply, "Does this fulfill my purpose?" Use your purpose to set your course in life.

17.

Affirm your life as though you already are all that you want to be. Learn to automatically turn your wishes into affirmations. Then start catching your negative thoughts, switch them around, and make affirmations out of them.

18.

Successful achievement requires three things—thoughts, feelings, and actions. Without all three, the pyramid collapses. If you have a dream that's not "making it," work on one (or more) of the sides of your pyramid.

19.

Don't accept the limitations of other people who claim things are undoable or unchangeable. If it's written in stone, bring your hammer and chisel.

20.

Let yourself make mistakes, admit them freely, and ask not "Who's to blame?" or "How can I hide this?" but "What's the lesson here? How can I do this better?" The goal is excellence, not perfection.

21.

Guilt is anger directed at yourself—at what you did or did not do. Resentment is anger directed at others—at what they did or did not do. Decide what expectation about yourself or another has been violated. Then change your expectation to conform to reality.

22.

Accept what you should and shouldn't have done, your future transgressions, and the present situations that you can't change. When you _can_ change something, do so.

23.

Replacing a negative memory with a positive one heals it. First you must let the negative memory fully play itself out in your inner sanctuary. Feel the emotions the memory produces.

24.

After a negative memory has played itself out in your imagination, let the image fade. What do you wish had happened? See it. What would you like to have felt? Feel that.

25.

You can't blame the past for what you do today. That's like blaming gravity for the glass you broke. Just clean up the mess and get another glass from the cupboard.

26.

Relationships are amazing mirrors. When you hate someone, ask yourself, "What does this person remind me about myself that I hate?" When you love someone, ask yourself, "What does this person remind me about myself that I love?"

27.

Do what you fear doing. Tell yourself the fear is here—with its gift of energy and heightened awareness—so you can do your best and learn the most. Fear is not a wall; it's just an emotion. Walk through the fear.

28.

Increasing self-esteem is easy:
do good things and remember
that you did them. You're great!

29.

If you refuse to feel the pain of loss, some of your ability to experience life becomes frozen. When you open yourself to healing, the "frozen" areas can "thaw." Love yourself enough to go through the healing process.

30.

Pain—emotional, physical, mental—has a message: "Your life would be more alive if you did more of this" and "Your loving would be more lovely if you did less of that." Let your pain speak. Follow its advice and you will be healed.

31.

Experience life as fully as water experiences a hand—surrounding and enfolding it. Then let go. Though water leaves some of itself on the hand (just as you leave some of yourself with the people and things you touch), the hand could no more hold the water than the water could hold the hand.

32.

Laugh—out loud and often.
Laughter is good for you.
Crying is also a marvelous
release. Tears are a natural part
of the healing process—and of
the enjoyment process, as well.
Allow yourself to be moved by
life.

33.

There is no end to joy, no upper limit. Discover that your capacity to know joy is as limitless as joy itself.

34.

Consciously be grateful for the good in your life. Make lists. Have gratitude flings. Be thankful for little things, big things, <u>every</u> thing. An attitude of gratitude is a great, full feeling.

35.

When you learn to give to yourself so fully that your cup overflows, then you may be called to be of service. Sometimes it's a hug, a kind word, or the right bit of information at the right moment. Perhaps it's a smile, a laugh, or a tear. Serve joyfully.

36.

Love is God's unconditional positive regard. Your core—your very being—is love. Share that love with yourself and others. Make love a verb.

37.

Life cannot be wrapped up in a string and handed to you as a tidy package. Life is a process. The surprise continues. Enjoy!

Books Available from Prelude Press

Life 101: Everything We Wish We Had Learned About Life In School—But Didn't, $5.95

You Can't Afford the Luxury of a Negative Thought, $5.95

DO IT! Let's Get Off Our Buts, $5.95

LOVE 101: To Love Oneself Is the Beginning of a Lifelong Romance, $11.95

Prelude Press
8159 Santa Monica Boulevard
Los Angeles, CA 90046
1-800-543-3101

Lisa O. Engelhardt is editorial director for One Caring Place/Publications at Abbey Press. She is the author of *Acceptance Therapy*, *Happy Birthday Therapy,* and *Finding the Serenity of Acceptance.*

Illustrator for the Abbey Press Elf-help Books, **R.W. Alley** also illustrates and writes children's books. He lives in Barrington, Rhode Island, with his wife, daughter, and son.

The Story of the Abbey Press Elves

The engaging figures that populate the Abbey Press "elf-help" line of publications and products first appeared in 1987 on the pages of a small self-help book called *Be-good-to-yourself Therapy*. Shaped by the publishing staff's vision and defined in R.W. Alley's inventive illustrations, they lived out author Cherry Hartman's gentle, self-nurturing advice with charm, poignancy, and humor.

Reader response was so enthusiastic that more Elf-help Books were soon under way, a still-growing series that has inspired a line of related gift products.

The especially endearing character featured in the early books—sporting a cap with a mood-changing candle in its peak—has since been joined by a spirited female elf with flowers in her hair.

These two exuberant, sensitive, resourceful, kindhearted, lovable sprites, along with their lively elfin community, reveal what's truly important as they offer messages of joy and wonder, playfulness and co-creation, wholeness and serenity, the miracle of life and the mystery of God's love.

With wisdom and whimsy, these little creatures with long noses demonstrate the elf-help way to a rich and fulfilling life.

Elf-help Books

...adding "a little character" and a lot of help to self-help reading!

New Baby Therapy
#20140 $4.95   ISBN 0-87029-307-9

Grief Therapy for Men
#20141 $4.95   ISBN 0-87029-306-0

Living From Your Soul
#20146 $4.95   ISBN 0-87029-303-6

Teacher Therapy
#20145 $4.95   ISBN 0-87029-302-8

Be-good-to-your-family Therapy
#20154 $4.95   ISBN 0-87029-300-1

Stress Therapy
#20153 $4.95   ISBN 0-87029-301-X

Making-sense-out-of-suffering Therapy
#20156 $4.95   ISBN 0-87029-296-X

Get Well Therapy
#20157 $4.95   ISBN 0-87029-297-8

Anger Therapy
#20127 $4.95   ISBN 0-87029-292-7

Caregiver Therapy
#20164 $4.95   ISBN 0-87029-285-4

Self-esteem Therapy
#20165 $4.95   ISBN 0-87029-280-3

Take-charge-of-your-life Therapy
#20168 $4.95   ISBN 0-87029-271-4

Work Therapy
#20166 $4.95   ISBN 0-87029-276-5

Everyday-courage Therapy
#20167 $4.95   ISBN 0-87029-274-9

Peace Therapy
#20176 $4.95   ISBN 0-87029-273-0

Friendship Therapy
#20174 $4.95   ISBN 0-87029-270-6

Christmas Therapy (color edition)
#20175 $5.95   ISBN 0-87029-268-4

Grief Therapy
#20178 $4.95   ISBN 0-87029-267-6

More Be-good-to-yourself Therapy
#20180 $3.95   ISBN 0-87029-262-5

Happy Birthday Therapy
#20181 $4.95   ISBN 0-87029-260-9

Forgiveness Therapy
#20184 $4.95   ISBN 0-87029-258-7

Keep-life-simple Therapy
#20185 $4.95   ISBN 0-87029-257-9

Be-good-to-your-body Therapy
#20188 $4.95   ISBN 0-87029-255-2

Celebrate-your-womanhood Therapy
#20189 $4.95   ISBN 0-87029-254-4

Acceptance Therapy (color edition)
#20182 $5.95   ISBN 0-87029-259-5

Acceptance Therapy
#20190 $4.95   ISBN 0-87029-245-5

Keeping-up-your-spirits Therapy
#20195 $4.95   ISBN 0-87029-242-0

Play Therapy
#20200 $4.95   ISBN 0-87029-233-1

Slow-down Therapy
#20203 $4.95   ISBN 0-87029-229-3

One-day-at-a-time Therapy
#20204 $4.95   ISBN 0-87029-228-5

Prayer Therapy
#20206 $4.95   ISBN 0-87029-225-0

Be-good-to-your-marriage Therapy
#20205 $4.95   ISBN 0-87029-224-2

Be-good-to-yourself Therapy (hardcover)
#20196 $10.95   ISBN 0-87029-243-9

Be-good-to-yourself Therapy
#20255 $4.95   ISBN 0-87029-209-9

Available at your favorite bookstore or directly
from us at: One Caring Place, Abbey Press
Publications, St. Meinrad, IN 47577.
Or call 1-800-325-2511.